DRIVE THROUGH THE NIGHT

Selected Poems by

Frank Perero

PAGE PUBLISHING
Conneaut Lake, PA

First originally published by Page Publishing 2022

ISBN 979-8-88654-293-6 (pbk)
ISBN 979-8-88654-294-3 (digital)

Printed in the United States of America

AUTHOR'S STATEMENT

Nothing in life occurs in a vacuum. Every thought, every word, every deed is incumbent upon an equal thought, word, or deed for its genesis. The characters and situations you will encounter in this collection do not stand alone. They come to life only because your thoughts are so vivid. My earnest hope is that you may see yourself in some of these poems. If you do, welcome to the ship of hope and redemption. We are waiting for you. It's a big ship.

Acknowledgments

I wish to thank the following:

My family, especially my mother and Uncle Bobby.
The Italian American Writers Association and Board Members
Gil Fagiani, Maria Lisella, and Bob Agnoli for
your support and encouragement.
The Last Wednesday Reading Series at Rocky Sullivan's
and their curator the late Lisa McLaughlin.
Seven Towers Press in Dublin for previously publishing
Drive through the Night and *Sophocles.*
Catherine McWeeney for your superb editing and
invaluable contributions to the creative process.
Larry Kirwan for your support and the inspiration
I've garnered from your work.
Joe Hurley for your support and
encouragement from the beginning.
A special thank-you to Chris Byrne and Rocky Sullivan's
for your support and inspiration over the years.
All of my friends and acquaintances who have influenced
my sensibility, resulting in these snippets of real life.
And finally thanks to Nancy Liu for your support and long-ago
designation of me as the "people's poet." I never forgot that.

DRIVE

DISTANCE

CONFLICT

CONCORD

DRIVE

DRIVE THROUGH THE NIGHT

Her image has faded the last couple of weeks,
a ghastly outline is all that remains.
And when her memory is forever erased,
new photos will appear in my mind's picture frame.
That day, though, is a long time from now,
so I'll patiently wait for each dawn's new light.
And the only way for me to survive
is to jump in my car to drive through the night.

Sometimes it feels I'm the only one living,
a speck of light in the distance to focus on.
And I still have a good four or five hours,
to see if my solitude will outrun the dawn.
Most times it's lonely I start seeing mirages,
as I mix a concoction of self-doubt and fright.
Yet somehow, I know what it is I am missing
can only be found if I drive through the night.

The night is forgiving as the day never is,
for only the brave will tempt the night's wrath.
And if you just make it through those few cursed hours,
the dawn will reveal a brilliant new path.
But the day's path is littered by those beaten down,
Defiled, and bloodied by an indiscriminate life.
They all tried their best but died never knowing
the only way to survive is to drive through the night.

Melodious Life

You've encountered rough weather and are so ill-prepared,
you'll be blown to oblivion in a couple of steps.
You're spinning your wheels and cursing your fate,
and the thing is you haven't seen the worst yet.
You wonder where day is or is darkness forever,
could it all be a symptom of all you've done wrong?
No, you steady your gait and then force a smile,
it's but a different refrain of the same song.

As children, we're taught all of the lessons,
it forms the essence of who we are now.
And my father worked—he never relented,
I became who I am by the sweat of his brow.
See, some learn perseverance and others regret,
some feel like outsiders and others belong.
And some sense they're falling off a cliff,
when it's only a different refrain of the same song.

My state of mind can change twenty times in a day,
the perils of not taking medication.
And the most valuable lesson I learned from my dad,
was the lesson of determination.
See, you gotta keep going when the day becomes daunting,
and the nighttime just lasts too goddamned long.
'Cause whatever we encounter in this melodious life,
is but a different refrain of the same song.

Sign of Life

The shops are closed, the streets deserted,
downtown is living up to its name.
Any sign of life has dissipated,
and in its place is gut-wrenching pain.

So you turn the corner, pull up your collar,
in time to face a wicked breeze.
And if you were a praying man,
you would drop right down to your knees.

Brand-new to town but not to the night,
you've been fighting it all your life.
And it doesn't matter the town you're in,
it's always the same—the dreaded night.

You'd pay a lot for a smile—even more for a friend,
but there is no kindness going around.
So you tuck your scarf into your coat,
just one more night in one more town.

As you cross the bridge that leaves downtown,
you can see your breath dance in the air.
For you, at least, a sign of life,
but you know, no one is there.
You were always taught to look both ways,
and always have learned wrong from right.
But they never taught you how to cope,
with the cursed, endless night...

WRITER'S KISS

Have you ever loved something so much,
that it pulsated and bled in your hands?
Have you felt the might of the universe,
was meant for you to command?
Well, that's how I feel when I put pen to paper,
and begin composing any preamble.
We all serve our passions and writing is mine,
it's my lover, my whore, and my gamble.

I've been traveling a road devoid of all light,
So I give thanks for the moon every mile.
And that's how I feel when I am with you,
they're the same; the moon and your smile.
They provide me with hope when I'm lost in the dark,
without the strength to light a candle.
But as sweet as you are, my writing comes first,
it's my lover, my whore, and my gamble.

I always see clearly when I'm here with myself,
there are no obstacles obstructing my vision.
And a long time ago, Rebecca once told me,
I shouldn't kiss her without her permission.
I'm not sure how I answered, I was probably mean,
when my response could have been simple.
I should have told her my writing's my kiss,
as well as my lover, my whore, and my gamble.

Fond du Lac

My mind's been rekindling so many memories,
soaking them up like a sponge.
And as I suspend the past and the future,
I dutifully examine each one.
And when a memory reaches the front of my brain,
I do my best to send it right back.
Then in a flash, I send myself reeling,
when I think of the girl from Fond du Lac.

Memories will haunt the old and the young,
hard to say whose demons are worse.
But those ghosts of regret are sure democratic,
they levy equal the weight of their curse.
And my demons now are much more intense,
one of life's psychological facts.
'Cause I still see her face after all of these years,
the face of the girl from Fond du Lac.

I'm thinking of taking a trip to Wisconsin,
meet my demons square on their turf.
Once and for all, I'll bid adieu to those ghosts,
and hopefully to all of the hurt.
But how sad it is after all of these years,
my psyche is stalled on that one track.
But I don't blame myself, and I don't blame circumstance,
I blame the girl from Fond du Lac.

CERTAIN SCARS

I was sleepy from doing nothing all day,
and watching the hours pass by.
I was tired of seeing the same damn sun rise,
and then set in that same damn sky.
Something had to give sooner or later,
I couldn't let this fever rage on.
So in darkness of night, I jumped from my bed,
And by the dawn, I was gone.

I hopped in my car and rode toward the sun,
didn't want anything setting on me.
I had been feeling confined by my own skin,
but now I finally felt free.
I rolled down the windows, pumped up the music,
and took a good hold of the wheel.
I started to sense my heart opening up
after so long trying hard not to feel.

You can ride for a day or a hundred,
But you're not gonna change who you are.
'Cause some things torn can't be mended,
and you're not gonna heal certain scars.
No, certain scars have a life of their own,
you carry them with you till your dying day.
And you can hop in a car and drive toward the sun,
But certain scars just won't go away.

BUSTING LOOSE

I've been surveying the lay of the land like a hawk,
watching as people move in and out of their lives.
And the more that I look the more I'm aghast,
yet it shouldn't come as any surprise.
Everyone does what they must to survive,
caught in the chaos of life's maelstrom.
Yeah, the more that I look the more I can see,
everybody has something they try busting loose from.

It's easy to say it all starts with one's youth,
sadly though, those words are facts.
Any man can deny many a thing,
but never can he walk his youth back.
It will haunt you and drive you off the path,
you so pompously thought you were on.
And for all of your life, you never realize,
it's always your past you try busting loose from.

Oh! Aren't we frail, insecure beings,
doubling down when we've got nothing to bet.
Showing our best face to those we don't know,
we lie to ourselves—we have no honesty left.
And be it our youth or our pasts, our family or friends,
our jobs or the fear of what we may become.
Yeah, the more that I look, the more I am certain,
every last one of us has something we try to bust loose from.

LATE SUMMER DRIVE

These days of summer are winding down
so I'm trying my best to harness their joy.
I need to store a cache of good vibrations—
build a defense the winter won't ever destroy.
I'm ever alert and stare straight ahead
in readiness to face anything I might meet.
Yeah, these days of summer are dwindling down while
I take a late summer drive along indifferent streets.

The urgency I'm feeling I sense nowhere else.
Dawns come and go and people do too.
I feel like a madman racing the clock—
a would-be detective with nary a clue.
But the sun's high and lazy, and I pack my gear
to head for the shore in this late summer heat.
I roll up the windows. I blast the AC.
And I head to the shore over indifferent streets.

Every road you take has to lead somewhere
but you have to know where it is you are going.
I only hope on this late summer drive,
yeah, I only hope my madness ain't showing.
But I reckon, "Don't worry," 'cause nobody cares—
they're too busy making their own lives complete.
So I smile a wry smile and sing along to Rodriquez
on my late summer drive along indifferent streets.

LEVEL GROUND

Even if we slow down, our mind keeps on churning,
driving us far from where we ought to be.
And we have to live in that hinterland,
forsaking time and reality.
And mister, I've been there and go back now and then,
traversing the crags of darkness and light.
But I always get back to level ground,
where my spirit rises to human heights.

Sometimes, we don't think and say something stupid,
and we pay for those words over and over again.
In this insincere world, we lose trusted souls,
some of them family but most of them friends.
And we get lost in mirages of terror and wine,
falling through burning crevices with wild wolves all around.
And while some of us fall through infinity,
lucky ones get back to level ground.

If you don't want to die then don't think about it,
and don't count the ticks on that infernal clock.
Sooner or later, come clean with yourself,
give up being someone you know you are not.
No, the deck isn't marked; the game isn't fixed,
this life's filled with beauty, it just has to be found.
And if you're too high or too low, the secret is simple,
get yourself back to level ground.

EAST VILLAGE TRAFFIC

Anna sure is resplendent in her East Village look,
sitting alone on a bench in Tompkins Square Park.
She flicks off the ashes while turning the page,
engulfed in the comfort of her poetry book.
A cold autumn wind runs down her spirit,
chilling her insides from her head to her toes.
But Anna sits back and smiles, content in the knowledge,
that she knows something nobody else knows.

Along Avenue A, a line starts to form,
either a celebrity shoot or just a free meal.
As a potpourri of emotion wraps 'round your brain,
it's hard to recognize what it is that you feel.
So you turn up your collar and dart through the park,
while your apprehension continues to grow.
But then you spy Anna in her elegant cool,
and can tell she knows something nobody else knows.

The night comes on quickly when you aren't prepared,
for all of the arrows life's aiming at you.
And in the grips of your fever, it's so hard to know,
just what it is you're supposed to do.
But the sweet strands of Christmas are filling the air,
as the East Village traffic moves endlessly slow.
Then in a moment of clarity, you start walking toward Anna,
because both of you know something nobody else knows.

21ST-CENTURY NEW YORK

I'd like to speak in early nineteenth-century language,
hide away in a castle in Leeds.
Ride into the city on weekends,
and cavort just like Byron or Keats.
Lie in the sunshine on a Sunday in May,
gazing up at that old London Tower.
But alas here I am in twenty-first-century New York,
making my way to happy hour.

I'd like to write in early nineteenth-century language,
have the beauty of nature imbue every word.
Let eloquent sentences teem from my pen
and compose an ode to the hummingbird.
Open my heart and let thoughts of you
unlock all of my passions.
But alas, here I am in twenty-first-century New York,
jotting down notes on barroom napkins.

I'd like to read in early nineteenth-century language,
let romantic words roll off my tongue:
"Leave thee, naked to laughter,
When leaves fall, and cold winds come."

Let me meet an early nineteenth-century lady,
adopt her as my muse.
But alas, here I am in twenty-first-century New York,
reading the sports pages of the *Daily News*.

DISTANCE

POINT IN THE DISTANCE

I'm focused on a point in the distance,
I can't tell you how far it is.
But that's where my spirit feels it should be,
it should be there wherever that is.
See, I've been itching to bust right out of my skin,
to land in a new time and place.
So I'm focused on that point in the distance,
as I contemplate my escape.

I'm obsessed with that point in the distance,
thing is I'm not sure it really is there.
It's probably my mind playing tricks,
and yet I sit here and stare.
I imagine hovering above it,
embracing all that I see.
I'm focused on a point in the distance,
wherever that point may be.

Think I'll try getting to that point in the distance,
but I don't believe I'll succeed.
I'm a slave to those things I cannot control,
my fears, my regrets, and my needs.
So that point in the distance will haunt me,
like some unholy curse.
Because I see it there but I know I won't reach it,
and can you think of a punishment worse?

THE LONELY SHIP

A lonely ship on the horizon
suddenly comes, into my vision.
It glides right through the setting sun
smooth as a surgical incision.
I watch it for one moment—two
the wind is gusting up a storm.
A lonely ship in all its grace
I know won't be here long.

The lonely ship is in full throttle,
though I sense it's not in any rush.
I wish I knew its manifest.
I almost can reach out and touch.
That lonely ship will soon be gone,
Will disappear right from my view.
I wonder if that ship can tell,
Those stranded here are lonely, too.

The lonely ship has disappeared,
I fear it wasn't ever there.
I slowly gather up my wits,
then take one final, squinting stare.
I get up to leave and head for the shore,
a soothing shadow begins to cast.
I judge an hour of sunlight left—
I wait for other ships to pass.

THE GENERAL

My head is swimming in morphine.
I'm numb from head to toe.
I can't tell one limb from another, are my legs even there?
I don't even know.
Chaplain tells me war has two rules:
Soldiers must fight and sometimes soldiers fall.
The nurses are saying we'd better get ready,
get ready for when the General calls.

My sister sent me a box of Godivas,
It's finished; I shared it with all of the guys.
Jenkins just got a new pair of legs,
but what can they do about O'Malley's eyes?
The days drag on one into another.
All we do is stare at the sanitized walls.
This morning they gave them an extra good cleaning,
Everything must be perfect when the General calls.
I won't be going home for a while,
most of us here are in for a long stay.
We're in what they call acute extended care,
where we revisit our misery day after day.
Today they told us we'd better snap to it,
make sure we shave—sit up straight and tall.
They want us looking our best for the photos,
the photos of when the General calls.

Dark Afternoon

My wheels keep on turning—they're on perpetual steam,
I'm looking forward—won't dare turn around.
Finally, my head is out of the clouds,
I'm on terra firma, planted square on the ground.

A new chapter's beginning, I burned all the rest,
and I can feel redemption coming upon me real soon.
But today I've lost all of my focus,
in the throes of a dark weekday afternoon.

The morning dawns bravely, and I follow suit,
so much to contemplate as I start my day.
And mister, I tell you those pains of our youth,
as much as we try, just don't fade away.
No, we carry them with us through this blessed life,
leaving us crazy and drunk, howling up at the moon.
Most times these pains come back to haunt me,
when I think too much on a dark afternoon.

The dunes of my youth are forever erased,
and my boardwalk of innocence has been blown to bits.
As is the shoreline where I used to write
and the 101 Street bench where I used to sit.
Today I thought about "The Pretender,"
in my youth, at the beach, 'twas our signature tune.
And it feels like December near ten in the evening,
but it's only November on a dark afternoon.

A GOOD DAY

There are many ways for you to proceed,
as you stumble along this melodious life.
Many tricks for you to conjure up,
as you balance your spirit between dark and light.
There are many thoughts for you to embrace,
and even more for you to smother.
But in the end what it is you must do,
is just put one foot in front of the other.

We went treasure hunting when I was a kid,
with a map that we found in a cereal box.
We brought a pick and a shovel and something to eat,
I stashed a five-dollar bill in one of my socks.
When we came to the hill where the treasure was buried,
I was afraid to climb down so I turned to my brother.
"Don't worry, Frankie, you'll be all right,
just put one foot in front of the other."

Lots of things change but many more don't,
and some days, if I'm lucky, I don't hear the clock.
But now when somebody dies, I just shrug it off,
it's all becoming less of a shock.
On a good day, I don't think too much,
and above me, the stench of decay doesn't hover.
Yeah, on a good day I summon my courage,
to just put one foot in front of the other.

Join the Parade (For Rick Danko)

There's probably a storm brewing somewhere,
and the people are all boarding up.
And somewhere a man stands on the edge,
convinced that he's had enough.
And somewhere, someone beats themselves up,
over every mistake they have made.
And somewhere, in a sleepy upstate New York town,
they're having a parade.

I just saw a video of an old musical hero,
who died before his time.
He was besieged by fame and wreaked by drugs,
when he came to the end of the line.
I remember seeing him at the Tinker Street Tavern,
one of the best shows he ever gave.
I wish I could've hugged him and screamed in his ear,
"Rick, let's join the parade!"

Yeah, since that time I'm keeping the faith,
there's so much that's hard to believe in.
I go back each summer to that sleepy town,
it has an aura allurin' and pleasin'.
And when the sun goes down,
I sit by the lake and sip vodka with lemonade.
But I never stay late because in the morning,
I have to join the parade.

Merry-Go-Round

First off you must realize how precious life is,
if you don't, you'll live to regret it.
And the secret to life is what's been in the past,
my friend, you just have to forget it.
I tell you we're lucky just walking outside,
to marvel at every sight and each sound.
Our emotions ride on a roller coaster,
and this life is nothing but a merry-go-round.

Over the years, I've been the same person,
but at different stages perceived in different ways.
And it haunts me to think how a past state of mind,
inhibited my nights and squandered my days.
But you couldn't blame me; I hadn't a clue,
I was the young bon vivant about town.
Sure, first bon vivant and then bon vi-nothing—
this life is a goddamned merry-go-round.

I met an old dude about three in the morning,
he was mumbling into his Makers Mark on the rocks.
Said he was happy with the life he had led,
he had near fifty years on the New Jersey docks.
He reached in his pocket and pulled out a twenty,
asked the barman to buy us a round.
He clinked my glass and looked in my eye,
"This life ain't nothing but a merry-go-round."

THE PENINSULA

A shower of misery reigns on my door,
testing my faith and drenching my soul.
Pointing my psyche in different directions,
each ending place foreboding and cold.
It gets hard to explain, this turn of emotion,
is this all a dream or is my dream real?
But through it all, the Bishop assures us,
"Sometimes we hurt, but always we heal."

From the carnage, I see where two towers stood,
now just one hollow monument representing all those who died.
And here, on the peninsula, we endeavor to hope,
but when is it enough that our people have cried?
Now a solemn mass torches our spirit,
even as we hold onto our emergency meals,
And the words of the Bishop ricochet off the heavens,
"Sometimes we hurt, but always we heal."

Twenty-three of us perished, may the Lord bless their souls,
Eleven years ago, in that bloody inferno.
Now here we stand with our lives on the curb,
no one to turn to and nowhere to go.
So we walk to St. Thomas, with hope for the young,
praying they'll never learn what it is we all feel.
Then we blow out the candles and exchange the kiss of peace,
and hope we'll be able to heal.

Montauk Inn

I woke with a vengeance this morning,
startled to count the steps to the stars.
My vision was slicing clear into tomorrow,
all the way to Venus and Mars.
I felt light-of-being—out of my body,
without a future or past.
I exuded in life and the joy it could bring,
until I realized this feeling couldn't last.

I jumped in my car and pointed her east,
didn't want any sun setting on me.
Then in a moment of angst, I suddenly realized,
it's getting late to be whatever I wanted to be.
As my head started spinning, I swerved to the fast lane,
a torment inside pressed hard on the gas.
When I cleared the traffic, I caught my breath,
'Cause I realized this feeling was not going to last.

I wound up at an inn at the tip of Montauk,
no further to travel except back through the years.
With the fireplace crackling, I had a Guinness,
gently seasoned with the salt of my tears.
I leaned back on the sofa and started to mingle,
as "Cinnamon Girl" came on the PA.
I took a gulp and couldn't decide,
if this moment should last or just go away.

FISHING

Our dreams and goals are what make up a man,
but as I'm getting older my dreams start to ebb.
I still have the fire but the fire is different,
and that sense of defiance is leaving my head.
I still know who I am and what I must do,
I will never stop fighting against Father Time.
But at the moment my only goal,
my only dream is to get a fish on the line.

Legions before me and legions to come,
will battle the specter of a cruel setting sun.
But faith is a virtue and hope springs eternal,
I'll need them both in the struggle to come.
It's a struggle of wills and a war of resilience,
waged by the heart of the universe, on mine.
And I know tomorrow I'll have time to plan,
so today all I want is to get a fish on the line.

You can go through a lifetime with all those you meet,
and never discuss one idea of substance.
And I've been famous for when it goes wrong,
to chalk it up to circumstance.
Ah, but I was young and eager and foolish,
ignoring the truths on all the road signs.
But there's always time to fix things right,
and I'll start out by getting a fish on the line.

SAILBOAT

There is so much to do yet so little time,
so much to see but not enough gumption.
And the rules of engagement, I've always championed,
I only can hope someday will mean something.
No, I can't change the world, idealistically, I've tried,
I have trouble changing the brand of my toothpaste.
I'd give a ransom if only I could catch up
to some of the dreams I have chased.

I am right on the cusp of enlightenment and death,
the pole position in the race of my life.
It's so very easy to be compromised,
and almost impossible to stand up for what's right.
And carrying the weight for all that is righteous,
can split a good man straight down the seams.
The only thing that keeps me going,
is the prospect of realizing all of my dreams.

The week between Christmas and New Year
is a most welcome pause in the game.
No one is looking and no one is pushing,
no one has the want to google your name.
Time for reflection and time for a pint,
time to contemplate what this crazy life means.
Time to place all your faith in a sailboat,
to summon your courage and set out for your dreams.

CONFLICT

Modern Times

I have a friend who wishes she was born in the '20s,
these modern times just tear her apart.
She's got a heart that's true as gold,
too bad we can't pay the bills with our heart.
She's been lied to and cheated and hung out to dry,
perceived as different for just being kind.
She's got a heart as true as tomorrow,
yeah, she just wasn't meant for these modern times.

All that we need is at the tip of our fingers,
at the tip of our cell phone or another device.
I have been thinking about that Robert Frost poem,
would you rather die from fire or ice?
Every situation has its own special truth,
but to their own truth, many people are blind.
And sadly, the truth is that so many people,
just weren't meant for these modern times.

Everything changes an eon a minute,
religion and family—everything about this life.
Just keeping up with the changes,
can condemn a good man to eternal night.
And I know the score, I've been long at the game,
I'm finely in tune with the rhythms and rhymes.
And that's why I wish I was born long ago,
I just wasn't meant for these modern times.

Dark and Light (A Christmas Wish)

That infernal clock keeps ticking,
the incessant sun dawns every day.
This fleeting life overwhelms my being,
and leaves me numb with nothing to say.
But my end-of-year reprieve has come,
for this moment my heart can cheer.
This fleeting life overwhelms my being,
I'm thankful Christmastime is here.

No man is an island, I heard that first,
many years ago in my vibrant youth.
But sadly, I just shrugged it off,
I was too young and stubborn to hear the truth.
I realize now we all need the comfort
of other people to ward off our fear.
Yes, we need the warmth of other people,
we remember that when Christmastime is here.

We spend too much time in our own realms,
our minds combust with spirits scorched.
That is when the unheard-of happens,
a good man condemned by his own thoughts.
It's a ruthless, timeless, endless struggle,
that leaves you trapped between your needs and fears.
A universal struggle of dark and light,
be thankful Christmastime is here.

Familiar Face

Sometimes in a crowd, I still feel alone,
people coming and going, yet I'm standing still.
With a hole in my soul where the wind's blowing through,
a hole in my soul that nothing can fill.
If the crowd slows down, I do the same,
if they speed up, I pick up the pace.
And all the while I don't ask much for much,
all that I seek is a familiar face.

The baker downstairs is missing your smile,
and the man on the train is a stranger to me.
This endless procession of forms, I don't know,
is taking me somewhere I don't want to be.
Down a dark road where I feel alone,
a desperate, dark foreboding place.
And yet I don't ask for much,
all that I seek is a familiar face.

There are three billion people or so I hear,
Yet I know the faces of so very few.
I look in the vacuum of every last one,
and every last one I imagine is you.
But no, you are gone and as I'm on my own,
I pray to find a life-saving grace.
So I continue on life's lethal road,
searching only for a familiar face.

THE PEOPLE I MEET

I've been looking for somewhere to direct my anger,
I need to get it off of my chest.
I have to funnel all my frustration,
to get it out of my system so no frustration is left.
I'm looking for somewhere to deposit the trash,
that builds up inside me on these city streets.
And I want to, just once, look in their eyes and smile
as I gaze at the faces of the people I meet.

I need to rid myself of all the bad thoughts,
that fill up my head polluting my brain.
And I want to make sure that all of life's dirt,
is washed from my soul and won't leave a stain.
I need to eject all of my stress,
to relax at night if even just for a while.
I need to gaze at the faces of the people I meet,
and then, just once, look in their eyes and smile.

I want to banish my doubt—get it out of my head,
and start to believe what I feel in my heart.
I need to make sure that song's always with me,
so I can sing it whenever I want.
And I need to extinguish all the bad memories,
it's only the good ones that I want to keep.
I want to, just once, look in their eyes and smile,
as I gaze at the faces of the people I meet.

Not Every Day

Sometimes you meet someone you can talk to,
when you are finally able to let down your guard.
Somebody without ulterior motives,
just cool conversation like you're in your backyard.
You talk about life and muse about love,
you await with eagerness what they have to say.
Yeah, sometimes you meet someone you can talk to,
but that's not going to happen to you every day.

Sometimes you look at yourself in the mirror,
and for once, you are pleased with what you see.
Sometimes you realize that fate's not absolute,
you are able to be whatever you wanted to be.
You have faith in humanity and faith in yourself,
and from your values, you will not stray.
I know sometimes you have faith in yourself,
but that courage won't come to you every day.

Sometimes you look at a colorless sky,
and all by yourself, you fill in the colors.
Sometimes you have unfathomable strength,
and never need to depend upon others.
Yeah, sometimes the world seems like it's your own,
you command every raindrop, every snowflake.
I know you have felt on top of the world,
and I know that feeling doesn't come every day.

THE OLD MAN AND CLANCY

Clancy has probably kept his old master alive,
being walked five times a day keeps them both strong.
But at nearly twenty, Clancy is no longer spry,
so he and his master sort of hobble along.
They walk just like lovers with that same lovers' gait,
as the old man, tightly, grabs hold of the leash.
We only spoke for a moment, but it was easy to see,
when he was with Clancy the old man was at peace.

"Aye, it's getting too hot for Clancy, we'd better get home.
I'll put a cold towel over his head.
I'll switch on the TV, lay out Clancy's food,
and then at about nine, we'll both go to bed."
That's when I looked away and bent down to pat Clancy,
and heard the old man say, "Have a good day."
I looked up to reply but he couldn't hear me,
the old man and Clancy were drifting away.

SAL THE BARBER

I tell you, Sal, I've been reeling
right down to the balls of my feet.
I'm tired of pushing, so tired of driving
but hey, a guy has to compete.
I guess that's why there are only two classes,
there are the haves and the have-nots.
And Sal, be careful, you're cutting too much,
just take a little bit off of the top.

You know, Sal, I've been out in the badlands,
where they rip out the hearts of innocent souls.
And I've looked in the eyes of everyone getting older,
and realized survival was their only goal.
And before she died, I promised to call my Aunt Mary,
I beat myself up because I forgot.
But Sally, be careful, you've known me for years,
just take a little bit off of the top.

You know Sal, I can't believe you're still here,
everything changes but still, here you are.
And it's soothing to know when I need a friend,
I don't have to go very far.
And, Sal, I don't who will be dying next,
thing is, it's becoming less and less of a shock.
But, Sal, be careful, you're cutting too much,
just take a little bit off of the top.

MICK MCCANN

We used to play softball together,
I knew his sister and his folks.
We would flip our baseball cards,
then put the winners in our spokes.
Whenever teams were chosen up,
we'd wind up on the same side.
Then just tonight I got a call,
they told me Mick McCann had died.

We were exactly the same age,
about a year older than Mick's sister Chris.
I remember the night at Rockaway,
when I gave her, her first kiss.
I recall the summer moon was high,
as, on my chest, Chris laid her head.
Then just tonight I get this call,
they told me Mick McCann was dead.

I hadn't seen Mick in twenty years,
nor thought about him all that time.
But I always kept my dear friend's picture
in the deep recesses of my mind.
Then just tonight I saw that picture,
and to myself silently cried.
You see, just tonight I got this call,
they told me Mick McCann had died.

SOPHOCLES

I had left myself without cover,
there was no one to cover my back.
The backlog of memories was piling up,
my spirit and soul were under attack.
I tried forcing a smile but couldn't,
felt I was under some sort of hex.
I was always in control of whatever I did,
but now didn't know what to do next.

I stopped for a beer and downed it,
then ordered a shot on the side.
Felt like retreating into myself,
but there was no place we both could hide.
Grabbed hold of my senses and gave them a shake,
tried to get them all in a line.
Started to feel like a guy on the lam,
not wanting to go back to doing time.

I looked at my watch and saw it was late,
but no later than it was yesterday.
I thought of those times I should have said something,
but just didn't know what to say.
I refilled my beer then started talking
with some people in for the game.
They bought me a shot and then introduced
everyone in their group name-by-name.

I started to think about shots in the dark,
and just what is defined by success.
How every last person I trust in this world,
I can remember just how we met.
Then I thought of the future and Sophocles,

a lot of people don't know who that is.
And I realized the key to being happy,
is simply the people we surround ourselves with.

If you look real hard there's a path to the stars,
that leads to I'm not sure where.
But for all I am worth, everything that I am,
I guarantee the pathway is there.
All you need is your faith and a cold pint of beer.
It is so easy for hope to take leave,
so for every kind soul in the tangle of
doubt—I ask you just to believe.

BLOOD FROM A STONE

You can't turn back the hands of an uncaring clock
to relive all the days you might've lived wrong.
And you can't take an outcast of spirit and mind
and somehow make them feel they belong.
A lady can't feel like the belle of the ball
when she's spent too many evenings alone.
Forget about doing any of this,
it's easier getting blood from a stone.

It's a six-hour flight from New York to Madrid,
and you're not getting there any faster than that.
The truth won't come from politicians—
Independents, Republicans, or Democrats.
And hard as you wish, you're not erasing the name
carved, so perfectly, into the headstone.
Forget about doing any of this,
it's easier getting blood from a stone.

The uneducated and poor will never get justice
or receive adequate medical care.
And no one will ever hold your hand in your dreams,
you're left to yourself and your nightmare.
And no one is offering help to the vagrant,
as he sits in the cold rain, soaked to the bone.
So you have to forget about any of this,
it will be easier to get blood from a stone.

TRUCK

Sometimes it's hard to express just how I feel,
when my head is exploding from too much to drink.
And when I'm sitting alone in the blackness of night,
never mind how I feel, I can't even think.
I can't think about what might have been,
how a move here or there could've altered my luck.
But do you want to know how it is that I feel?
It's a little like getting hit by a truck.

How do I feel when I'm treading water,
and a life jacket is nowhere in sight?
And how does it feel when I can't fall asleep,
and I'm locked in a battle, just me and the night?
And how does it feel when I'm dodging life's arrows,
and I don't even have the desire to duck?
Please, let me try to explain,
it's a little like getting hit by a truck.

How do I feel when I think about her,
and when together, we got our first Christmas tree?
And how does it feel to finally realize
it's getting late to be whatever to be I want to be?
And how does it feel when I run out of gas,
and for a couple of months my spirit gets stuck?
It may be hard for you to understand,
but it's a lot like getting hit by a truck.

CONCORD

WARRIOR

Warriors line the pages of history,
proudly standing where heroes have stood.
Bravely defending those most at risk,
the weak, the helpless, and the misunderstood.
I take their lead in defending the honor,
of those spiritual outcasts caught up in life's war.
For all these I fight with a sternness of purpose,
my faith is my shield; my words are my sword.

Quick, come to the window, life's forces are massing,
waiting to mount, a vicious attack.
Advance scouts have been out searching for weakness,
at every corner and crossroad they're at.
We must remain diligent and must remain calm,
to compromise our emotions, which we cannot afford.
If we reason things out, we can defeat them,
our faith is our shield; our reason's our sword.

Predators line the streets where we live,
they conspire and block the paths that we take.
They're an arrogant band who too often find,
for all of their crimes, they never will pay.
But they're in my vision, I know who they are,
as I take a vow for your just reward.
And in the battle, I'll have the edge,
for my faith is my shield; and courage my sword.

UNSCATHED

The line that stretches from birth to the grave,
is frustrating and obtuse at best.
Every last minute of every last day,
confronts me with some sort of test.
I'm not sure how I'm doing as I dare not keep score,
I'm terrified of what I might see.
But all I know is that I took life's best punch,
and escaped with a bump on the knee.

I seem to be listening to all the old songs,
my thirst for what's new has been ebbing.
Though I strap on my courage as I do my seat belt,
most days I've no idea where I'm heading.
So I make a list of all whom I love,
and give thanks that my spirit is free.
And I pray that when I face judgment day,
the worst I come out with is a bump on the knee.

My emotional wounds just linger and linger,
long after the physical ones heal.
In the midst of my fever, I just can't convey,
to anyone how it is what I feel.
So I just turn the page and try to enjoy
a cold beer with the game on TV.
Then I put up my feet, feeling truly amazed,
that all I got is a bump on the knee.

TEETH

It's been a rough day, the cold won't relent,
I'm a man of summer trapped in winter clothes.
And though I have a plan and a destination,
I wander about with nowhere to go.
The warmth's going to help and a smile will too,
when I gaze at the faces of the people I meet.
But for the moment all I can do,
is zip my jacket and grit my teeth.

My state of mind can change in a bloody instant,
so I have to bank on the change yet to come.
And I used to be a man for the evening,
that was my playpen, the playpen of the young.
Now I wait for the morning, as I wait out the night,
as its ghastly visions dance all around me.
So at the moment all I can do,
is to say my prayers and grit my teeth.

I have no qualm with Father Time,
he's just doing his job like everyone else.
But trying to deal with his machinations,
makes me a blabbering shell of myself.
The cold and the night? They're easy pickings,
but Father Time will never accord me any peace.
So all I can do is count my blessings,
summon my courage and grit my teeth.

FINGERS AND TOES

I've been walking the highway with a backpack of memories,
wearing the cashmere scarf she gave me for Christmas.

It's a quarter-to-five and already it's dark,
what can I expect for the middle of winter?

I've been feeling all right and at times even strong,
though some days are hard—that's just how it goes.

I'm handling the winter and the separation,
except I don't have any feeling in my fingers and toes.

I met her in April or just after St. Paddy's,
I only know I was drunk, and she kissed really good.

And as the summer wore on, I forgot all about time,
else I would've stopped time completely; If only I could.

But time has to pass and the clock has to tick,
just as the river of time has to flow.

And on a dark road in Jersey, I'm feeling all right,
except I don't have any feeling in my fingers and toes.

It's just about a mile until I reach home,
my mile road mark is the 7-Eleven.

I might grab a coffee and pick up the paper,
then try to get a grip on just where I'm heading.

Yeah, I'm heading home—familiarity is safety,
but I keep a secret nobody else knows.

You see it's the middle of winter and I'm feeling all right,
except I don't have any feeling in my fingers and toes.

TICKING CLOCK

There are places and people who assuage your spirit,
there are things in this universe that make your heart light.
It's a constant struggle, trust me, I know,
and some days you're resigned to giving up on the fight.
But the equation is simple, and Mister it's certain,
we're all going to die it's just a matter of when.
Yeah, there are places and people who assuage your spirit,
your salvation lies in being surrounded by them.

People lash out when they're insecure about themselves,
they try to make you insecure too.
If you open your arms and reach out in this life,
you'll certainly find them, it's sad and it's true.
See, nothing is finite, there's no absolute,
the cavalry's not coming from over the bend.
But there are places and people who nurture your spirit,
Mister, you'd better get surrounded by them.

You have to stop counting those infernal ticks,
that emanate cruelly from that eternal clock.
As hard as I've tried, I learned I can't do it,
I just can't make that ticking stop.
So my sentence is life as it is for us all,
we've no other option but to see it through to the end.
But there are places and people who assuage my spirit,
and my quest has to be to get surrounded by them.

NEVER EASY

It never is easy to walk down the road,
you've been afraid to walk down in the past.
And it's never easy to let go of feelings,
you've always wanted to last.
And it's never easy to stand up to the ones,
you've always been taught to respect.
No, it's never easy to walk out the door,
and know just what to expect.

It never is easy to have a good friend,
and see the friendship suddenly end.
And it's never easy to make up a plan,
and know just how to begin.
And it's never easy to look at the sky,
and see nothing but stars.
It never is easy to live every day,
and not compromise the person you are.

It never is easy to rise from your bed,
when all you want is to sleep.
And it's never easy to paddle to safety,
when the water around's getting deep.
And it's never easy to give someone your soul,
without expecting the same in return.
It's never easy to know after all you've been through,
you still have so much to learn.

It never is easy to think back to your youth,
and not to be stung by the pain.
It's never easy to believe in your heart,
that all of us are the same.
And it's never easy for you to be strong,

to hold it when you want to cry.
And it's never easy to keep the same spirit,
when the years are passing you by.

No, it never is easy to face a new day,
when you know that death's hanging 'round.
And it's never easy to witness the fury,
and not be overcome by the sound.
No, it's never easy to navigate through,
the twisted maze and all of the strife.
No, it's never easy but you give it your best,
and just live this thing we call life.

LOVING FACES

My mind keeps on reeling from the infernal ticking,
and the incessant motion of time's carousel.
And as hard as I try, all I keep hearing,
is the hideous chorus of funeral knells.
I keep looking backward, God, what a curse,
balancing bravely on this breach I'm upon.
And, mister, I'm thinking back to my youth,
I only blinked once and man, it was gone.

A man's hopes and dreams bind him to the universe,
setting and then realizing his goals.
They are the essence of this fleeting life,
not realizing his dreams will gnaw at a man's soul.
And, mister, I realize all dreams are fluid,
but I can expect only so many new dawns.
I can't help but think about all of my dreams,
I only blinked once and God, they were gone.

This lifetime becomes one of anonymity,
because as we grow older our circle of acquaintances shrinks.
That's why I cherish each loving face,
so at least for a moment with this world, I'm in sync.
But those loving faces are beginning to shatter,
loving faces I used to so depend on.
And, mister, I tell you I stare at those faces,
then I blink once and all of them are gone.

Rest Stop

I keep plodding onward for little else I can do,
there's no magic elixir to set me up right.
Though I struggle to be a bold musketeer,
I stumble along like some errant knight.
My armor is pierced and my rapier blunt,
and my manner of jousting is long out of style.
But don't worry about me as I'll be all right.
all I need is to rest for a while.

I keep pushing onward to my just reward,
there's so much to do—but so little time.
And right now my focus just has to be,
on removing my fingerprints from the scene of the crime.
The crime is inaction—with constant thoughts of regret—and,
for my whole life, Mister, I've been on trial.
But before you decide if I'm guilty as charged,
I simply want to rest for a while.

Nothing is settled in a day or a week,
most things will linger till we're snug in the grave.
And of all of the virtues I've ever been taught,
the most valuable, surely, is we have to be brave.
But that's always easy; we too readily yield,
when our faith and conviction are lost in exile.
And, mister, I'm certain to get back my courage,
all I need is to rest for a while.

Daytime Stars

I'm banking on seeing tomorrow,
'cause I'm cruising clear through today.
I'm freeing myself from all the bad thoughts,
and those ghosts of regret and decay.
Hey, it's mid-December and sixty-five at the shore,
and I'm frolicking with nary a care.
I'm making a wish on daytime stars,
I can't see them, but I know they're there.

I'll be hunkering down for the holidays,
and might not emerge till St. Paddy's Day.
But I'll be thinking about those who nourish my soul,
and I'll smile when I envision their face.
Every morning I'll gaze at the sky,
and murmur a daytime prayer.
I'll make a wish on daytime stars,
I won't see them, but I'll know they're there.

Stars align in the sky each and every day,
they look down shedding blessings upon us.
They form a trajectory of wisdom and courage,
to a place that lies far beyond us.
So it's up to us, every moment we live,
to squeeze as much out of life as we dare.
And you gotta be sure to seek out daytime stars,
you won't see them, but trust me, they're there.

Day at the Beach

It's Monday morning at the shore,
the softest breeze caresses me.
The horizon calls out my name,
I stare into eternity.
I think about this crazy life—
all of the joys I don't realize.
I lean back in my easy chair
and slide my hat over my eyes.

A sudden squawk awakens me,
two gulls are fighting for a meal.
The children frolic by the shore—
they serenade with joyous squeals.
I feel free from worldly tension
could not feel sad, hard as I try.
I squint up at the torrid sun
and slide my hat over my eyes.

I leave the beach—secure a bench
I overlook all that is good.
My peace of mind is palpable;
I tap the bench to knock on wood.
I dream about a better world
without the pain, deceit, or lies.
I dream about a better world
then slide my hat over my eyes.

BLACK 47

It's a summer breeze on the first day of autumn,
and just for a moment, the world is all right.
I've forgotten about the battle I had,
with the man in the mirror that lasted all night.
Possibilities are boundless 'cause down here at the shore,
the sun is highlighting a pathway to heaven.
And so I recline just feet from the waves—
listening to a band called Black 47.

Our youth with our lives are forever entwined,
how old would you be, if you didn't know how old you are?
And on days I am feeling Father Time's wrath,
I unlock my prison and hop into my car.
I put her in gear and then floor the gas,
all of my dreams come alive and all my sins are forgiven.
I pop the sunroof and roll down the windows,
and put on a CD by Black 47.

People, places, and memories make up our lives,
they form the essence of just who we are.
And for every single, solitary memory,
all of us carry some sort of scar.
They remind us of our astounding journey,
and help us not make the same errors again.
But right now, I'm thinking about the happiest memories,
the memories of when I saw Black 47.

About the Author

Frank Perero, a lifelong resident of NYC, was educated at Queens College of the City University of New York with a BA in Creative Writing and at St. John's University with an MS in Rehabilitation Counseling.

His work has been published in numerous magazines and journals as well as corporate newsletters.

He has been actively working in local politics in NYC for the past eighteen years and was a candidate for the NYC Council in 2013.

This is the inaugural publication of a collection of his poetry.